Seasons of Solace

Reflections on Grief

Benjamin Allen

Rachel Flower

Written by Benjamin Allen
Photography by Rachel Flower
Edited by Deborah Louise Brown

ISBN: 978-0-9915397-3-4

The Invitation

Welcome. Within these pages is an invitation. Living with loss unfolds a unique landscape that resides within a common path. I invite you to go deep within the experience of loss itself and perhaps find a deeper experience of your own loss.

Through the years I have experienced one by one the death of my eight-month-old son, my wife, my thirteen-year-old son, my mother, and both of my brothers. Each loss brings up every loss. Nothing lives in isolation – neither my loss nor my love.

Each loss has shattered me, initially leaving me inaccessible to the world within me and to the world around me. Over and over I collected the pieces, I leaned into the depths of my separation and unexpectedly discovered what is at the very core of separation – connection.

I found this intertwining of loss, love and life by leaning into every shattered moment, every dark night and sunlit day. I followed my aloneness wherever it led and it has always led me to you.

Come sit with me and I will sit with you. In sitting next to each other within these pages of reflection, my hope is that our seasons of sorrow can rest gently into our seasons of solace.

For it is when I touch the very deepest part of me, I find you. It is when I cry out in my pain and separation that I can hear your cries of pain and separation. It is when I lean into everything that I can make my way into everything; and find you, too, leaning into your loss, your love, your life.

This is an invitation to lean into these pages. Perhaps, there we will meet and we will hear the echo of shattered hearts. We will embrace in both the shadow of sorrow and the illumination of love. And we will truly know that nothing lives in isolation, not our loss, not our love and not each other.

Welcome. You are not alone.

Benjamin

Autumn

Autumn resides between the warmth of summer and the bitter frost of winter. Shortened days give way to long cold nights. The landscape acquiesces to Autumn. The brilliant multicolored leaves have no defense against their impending demise. And neither did we.

It was Autumn that brought you to me. It was Autumn that took you from me.

I remember the first time I held you. The wholeness of our embrace completed the circle that had yet to unfold us. That first night when your hand held mine gave no warning, no sign, of the last night my hand held yours.

Autumn's transient nature unveiled the illusion of permanence. What was, is no longer.

I was helpless to stop the turning of the earth, the changing season. The axis of our embrace tilted beyond the tipping point and we fell into Fall. And now, I can no more move a mountain or push a river as I can turn back to the moment of our last embrace. The earth only moves in one direction and it is into Autumn I must go.

Death has separated our bodies, the rhythmic cadence of two hearts, leaving only one to beat, over and over one beat. Beating against Autumn. But until death has taken us both, both of us shall live. For love cannot be separated by any season, even Autumn.

If I could, I would lie down and let the blanket of multi-colored leaves cover my body as the earth has covered you. I would empty my Autumn into the same winds that carried you from me. I would go in search of you. But that is not my path. The path before me lies within me, deep within the recesses of unrelenting love, still in the curvature of time, still within the borders of space. Until I go there, my path is to be here.

As Autumn leans into Winter, I lean into you, into love, into loss, into life's fragments.

The inevitability of Autumn comforts me now. I embrace who I am to become from all that has come into my Autumn. I bow to what rises within me and will venture into wherever life leads me. And when I, too, find that earth's inevitable pull leans me against her bosom; and I, too, take flight, I will find you. For the more I find of me the more I find of you. And the more I find us in the inevitability of Autumn.

Loss has its own rhythm.

I let it draw me into its healing presence in the moment of its own choosing.

I no longer knew who I was.
I just didn't know who I had
become.

I know what used to be normal.
I just didn't know what the new
normal was.

All I knew was I didn't
know any more.

Healing is not an event.
Healing is in perpetual motion
unfolding what is in the midst of
what was and what will be.

Healing is not the end of my loss.
Healing is experiencing
the peace within my loss.

Just as there is no end to loss,
there is no end to healing.

There were times when I would go through massive
waves of sorrow. I just had to ride it out, go wherever
it led and end where it ended.

And when such waves subsided, I found within me an
expansion of the heart and a deeper way of relating to
loss, to life and to those I love.

My Afterloss has many layers.

*Some layers are filled with
footprints of others who grieve
and know the depths of sorrow.*

*But there are other layers
in my Afterloss landscaped
solely in solitude.*

*Trite sayings meant
to comfort only
compounded the
complexity
of my sorrow.*

*I needed silence
more than sound,
presence more than words.*

In a time of massive upheaval,
it is crucial to bring safe and
supportive people into my life.

When we lose someone we love,
we need love more than ever.
We need those that can be present,
helpful and understanding.

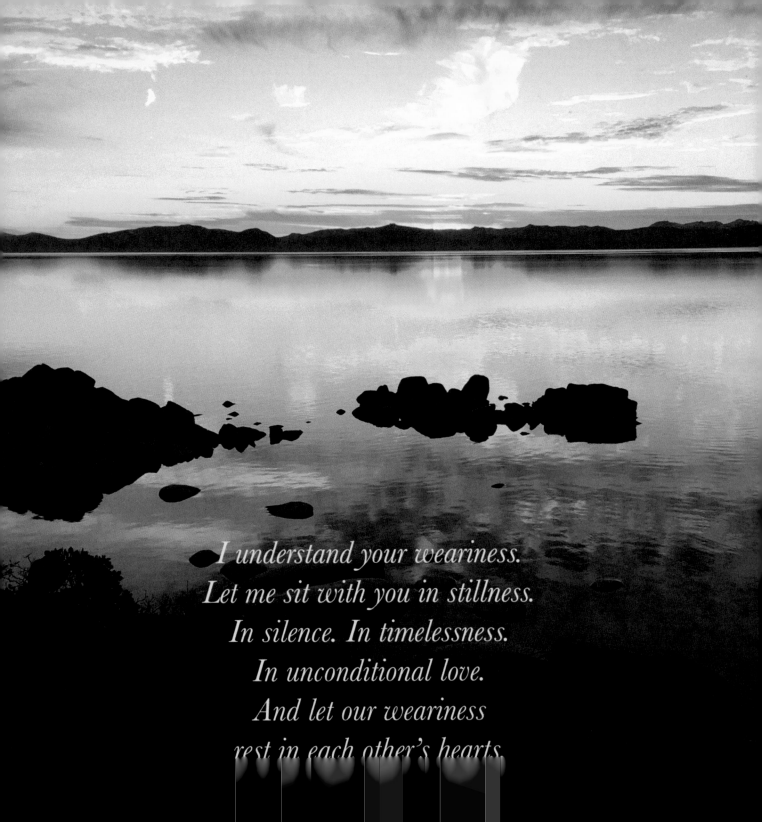

I understand your weariness.
Let me sit with you in stillness.
In silence. In timelessness.
In unconditional love.
And let our weariness
rest in each other's hearts.

*By candlelight I will go gently
into the Autumn night
and sit by my solitary flame.*

*I am clothed in camouflage
in order to disguise my Autumn.
The world around me cannot see
what Autumn has done to me.
The world has gone on
and I have gone in,
into the depths of loss,
of love, of life.*

It takes a broken heart to know how
to hold the brokenness of another.

I sought those that did not feel the
need to gather my brokenness.

I am so grateful for those that
simply gave presence to the pieces
that were left of me.

Am I the only one who cannot stop crying?
Am I the only one terrified of walking out
the door into a world turned
so strange and foreign?
Until I met you, I thought
there was only me, the only one.

I miss so much.
I miss their voices.
I miss our embrace.
I miss our laughter.

Beneath the surface,
I miss everything.

I go about my day
knowing that loss changes
everything,
especially what I miss.

Those that don't know great loss don't know what to say.

Those that do know the pain of great loss know there is nothing that can be said.

I am not the same.
Yet, I am not different.
This moment will always carry
that moment.

This day is the culmination of all days.
This tear has the trace elements
of all the tears I have shed.

*The only way for me
to get to my healing was
to go through my pain.*

*I unclenched my loss
and opened to whatever
came into my life.*

*What I thought was
going to kill me
was actually going
to heal me.*

Winter

The cold settled in way too quick, way too early, way too deep.

The empty days emptied me over and over. Winter did not descend upon me. Winter ascended from within me. Sunrise gave no promise of sunset. My voice could barely rise above a whisper. Winter gave little warmth to the inner landscape of my sorrow.

Frozen dreams lay barren in the distance between us.

The only ask I have ever wanted lies buried in the icy wasteland. I simply asked for one more day. Just one more day that did not end in night. One more breath. Just one more breath that did not end in exhalation. One more touch. Just one more touch that did not leave me so alone and unreachable.

Long gone is tomorrow. Long gone is yesterday. Long gone is today.

I wander the wilderness of Winter long gone. Each moment dissolves before I reach it, before it can reach me. I should be cold here, but I can only feel how much feeling is long gone. Gone. Gone. Gone. Where do I go when there is no place left to go?

I went the distance and found distance is all I have left. The distance of me to you. The distance of me to them. The distance of me to me. But I am still here. When did here become so distant?

Time haunts me in its metronome of moments.

They say time will heal. But in the depths of Winter, time simply echoes where time stopped, where time changed directions and where timelessness took our time. The beating of my broken heart keeps time, takes time, leaves time; then takes more time.

You returned to the place you came from, and I am left still with what little is left. When you entered my world, you entered me. The impenetrable was penetrated by your presence. Every day we were gifted to share, healed me.

I am cold now, weary and cold. I am alone in an overcrowded world of aloneness. I reach for you only to find the charred embers of me.

But Winter is just one season. Just as there will be more Winters, there will be more Springs, more Summers…and more Autumns. I will find you in every season. I will find there is more left of me from all you have left for me. For you left me the greatest part of you. Like a warm fire in Winter, you left me your love.

In the early days of loss,
everything hurt.
I had to find a way
to let my sorrow flow.

I had to lean into my pain
and give it expression,
or in my resistance,
I would have been totally
overtaken and destroyed.

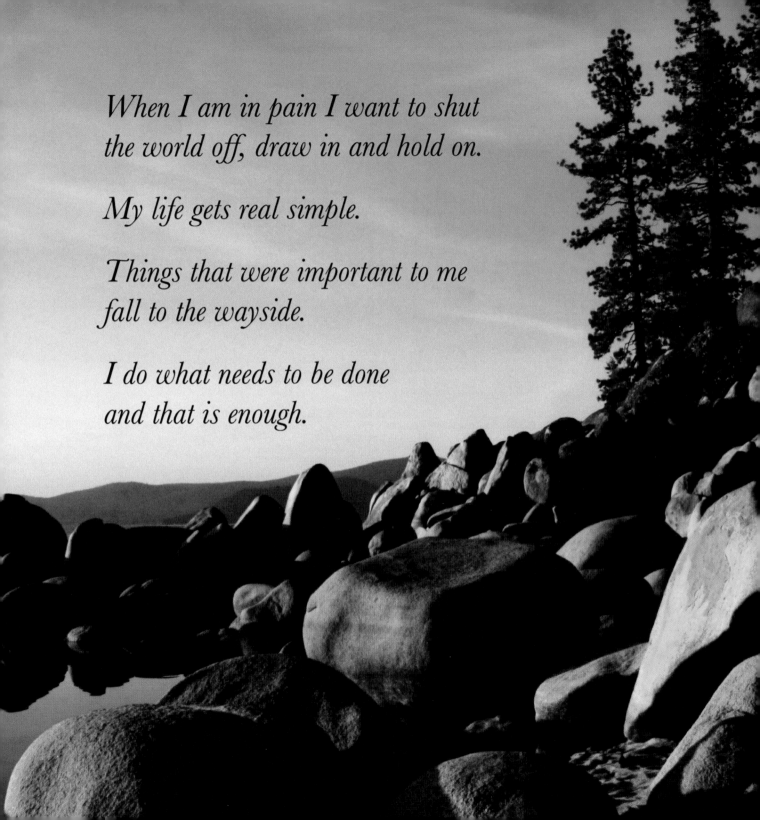

When I am in pain I want to shut
the world off, draw in and hold on.

My life gets real simple.

Things that were important to me
fall to the wayside.

I do what needs to be done
and that is enough.

Sometimes I just needed to be heard.
I needed someone to say, "I hear you.
And I'm here for you."

Those who did not try to take my pain
away were the ones who eased my pain.

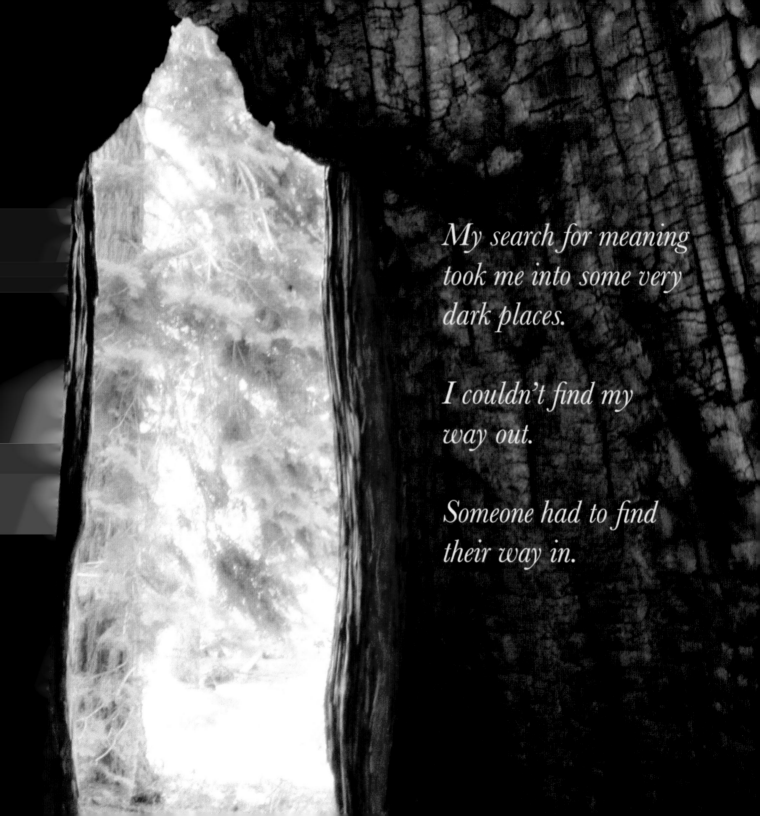

My search for meaning
took me into some very
dark places.

I couldn't find my
way out.

Someone had to find
their way in.

There are moments when I am absolutely incapacitated.

If the heart did not beat spontaneously there would be no beat at all.

In that moment I measure the distance by how far am I willing to go into this pain.

Am I willing to hold the fullness of love in the emptiness of my heart?

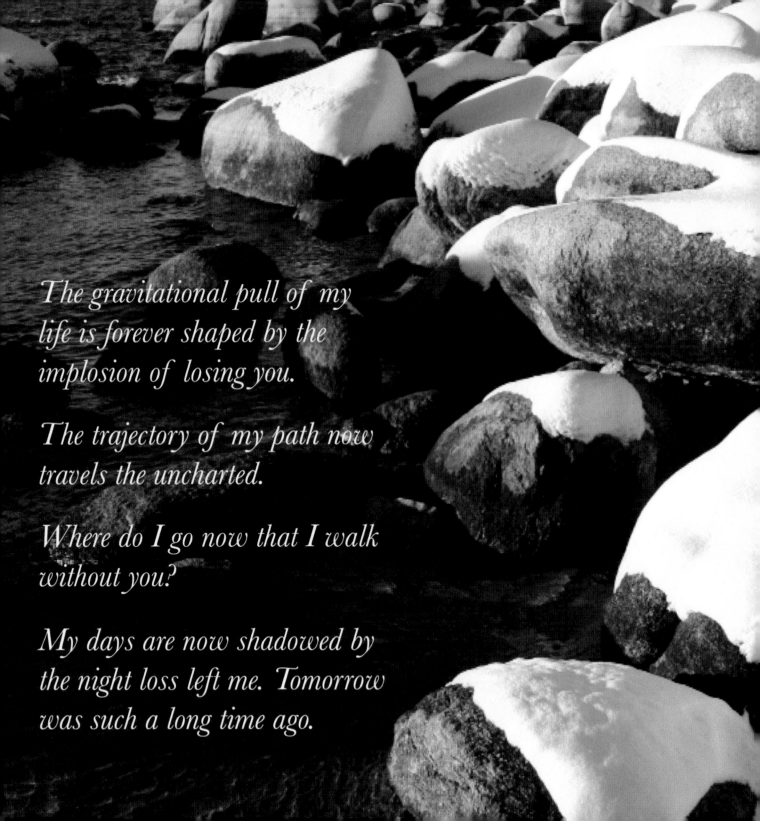

The gravitational pull of my
life is forever shaped by the
implosion of losing you.

The trajectory of my path now
travels the uncharted.

Where do I go now that I walk
without you?

My days are now shadowed by
the night loss left me. Tomorrow
was such a long time ago.

I was immobilized.

It looked to the world, and to me, that I was doing nothing.

But I was actually starting the process of reintegrating a new way of relating to life, to the one I loved and lost.

And to me.

And it took me a lot of doing nothing to do all that.

I have become grateful on those days
I simply can't do surface things.

It tells me I'm doing the deeper dance
of healing my sorrow.

My living in loss isn't a progression,
getting better and better.

My living in loss is a continual unfolding,
going deeper and deeper.

*We all need
someone who
can find us
when loss
leaves us lost.*

When I lost my beloved,
I thought I had lost love.

When I emptied into an empty world,
I thought love had emptied too.

But deep in the void,
At the very heart of the abyss,
There was the pulse of presence.

There, I found
What I thought I had lost.

*Memory seeps into the
present tense through a thought,
a smell, a song, a photograph, a word.
Anything and everything.*

*I am reminded daily of what is gone
and what is still here.*

The initial shock and horror that rips a life to pieces subsided into the task of finding what pieces are left, and figuring out what to do with them.

I wanted to be alone,
but not completely alone.

I wanted someone to sit
next to me in my solitude.

The Winter cold settled in way too quick,
way too early, way too deep.

Winter did not descend upon me.
Winter ascended from within me.

I look for you everywhere.
I stare into the ice of winter,
searching for your reflection.

But all I can see
is the reflection of someone
I no longer know.

Spring

Winter's hibernation dissolves into Spring's rejuvenation.

I am caught between two worlds. Spring beckons renewal and the moving of long nights into longer days. Night has been my refuge. It has been where I have retreated into all my loss, all my love, all of death, all of life. And now the world around me is calling. A part of me wants to stay tucked into Winter's long, long nights. But Spring wants to coax me into day, to join the world around me when there are times the world within me cannot reach that far.

How can I now fit in this strange and foreign world?

A part of me has gone with you and a part of you has now found residence in me. My world has been stretched across a universe into the infinite and now the finite asks me to move among them. There is simply not enough of this world to hold all that I am now.

The contraction of loss has given way to the expansion of love.

It is not about "going on." It is about going in, into a deeper relationship to the world around me and the world within me. The embrace of my loss leads me into greater life. The expanse that separated us is the same expanse that binds us in this moment, in every moment of life. I am a collection of all that we were, we are and we will be.

Spring is an offering of mountain snowcaps melting into the vitality of rivers and finding their way into the vast ocean of me. One drop becomes all drops. One moment becomes all moments. One journey becomes every journey. My entry into a day full of life is a reflection of our testament of inseparable love, a testament of loss's Spring.

Spring asks for all of me. I thought that in my sorrow I had been shattered to pieces and the fragments of me had been spread out across an infinite void. But as I have leaned into my Autumn and Winter, I now see a different unfolding. My shattered pieces are reshaping into a new me: and my new me begins where our love has never ended. The only vessel that can hold the infinite expanse of loss is the present moment in life.

I do not need to "do" the day. I simply need to be the moment. For it is in the moment that both loss and love unfurl me.

Spring's invitation is to dance and sing. What I thought I had lost has returned in unexpected ways. What was important to me once has melted away like Winter melts into Spring. I carry into each moment not only the gifts you have given me, but the gift of you within me. It is a new dance with new music. It is the song of Spring that sings me as I sing you.

I cannot change the past.

But the past has changed me.

I touch a memory,

and the memory touches me.

Memories hurt. Memories heal.

Memories tell me how far
I have come.

And how far I've yet to go.

*I return to the
sacred places of memory
to remind myself that
it is not my sorrow
that lives there.*

It is my love.

Illumination comes from
within my true, authentic self,
unfurling what I truly believe.

Whatever you believe,
please let it be the luminescence
that lights your path.

*I want to go as deep as I can into
the interior terrain of my life.*

*Everything is not out there.
Everything is in here.*

Just as the wind
shapes the rocks,
loss shapes me.

Breath by breath.

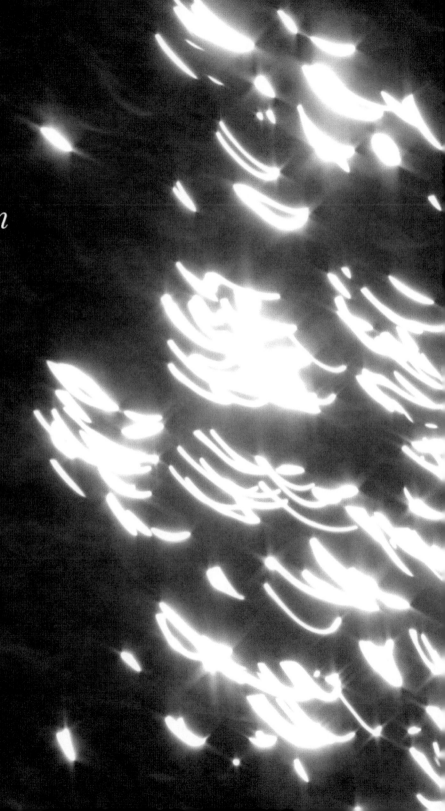

It takes a lot to swim
the depths of life.

Loss refuses
to let me skim
the shallow waters.

Deep calls to deep.

The tenderness I experienced with those
I have loved and lost never goes away.

Somewhere in the recesses
of this moment resides
every feeling,
every encounter,
every word,
every touch.

Everything.

When it rains, it rains.

The same rain that can destroy
life can also give life.

The same sorrow that can crush
me can also heal me.

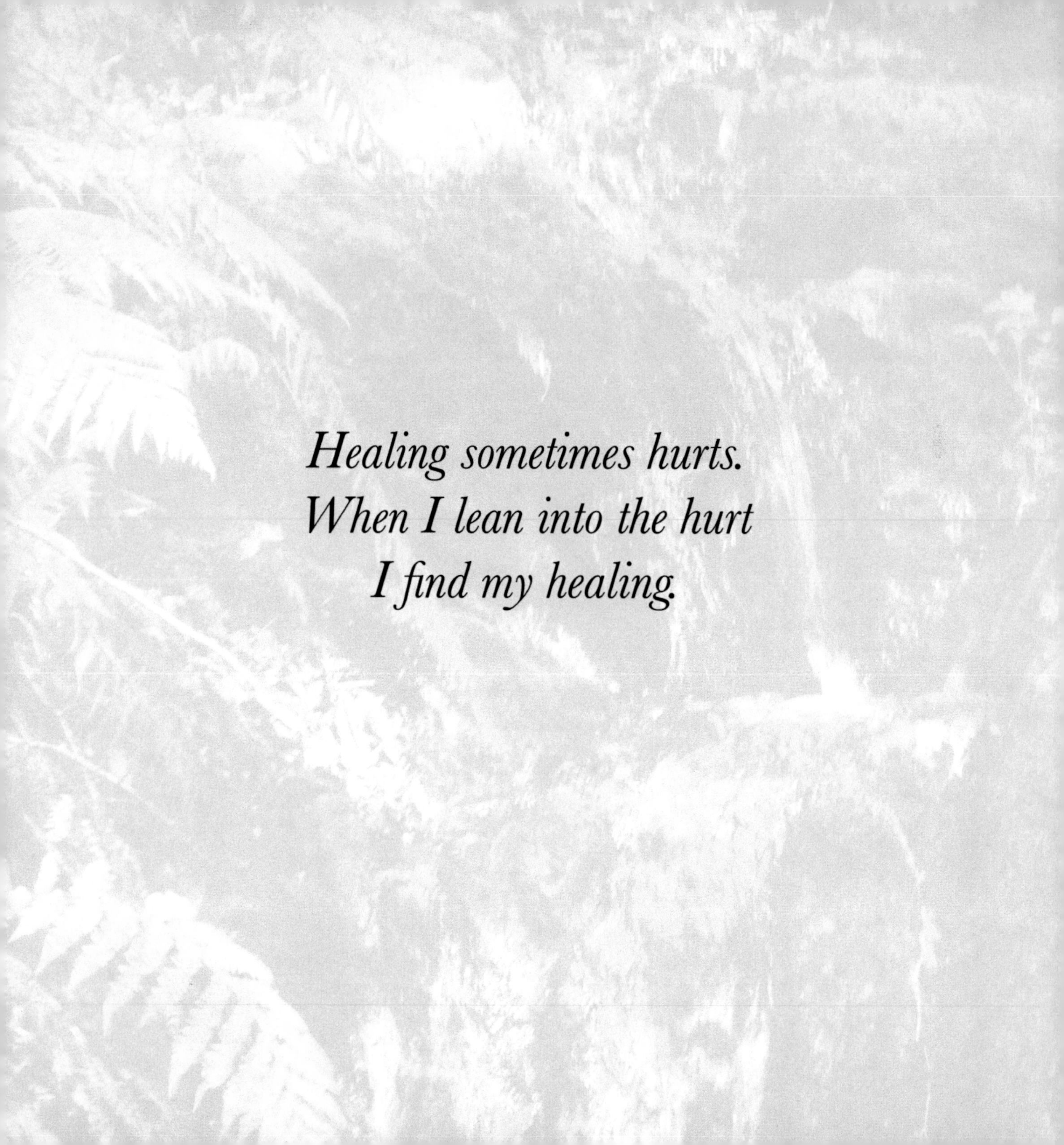

Healing sometimes hurts.
When I lean into the hurt
I find my healing.

Where can I harbor such sorrow?
In whom, in what, can a safe haven be found?
When there is nothing left to hold onto,
who will hold me?

*My experience of yearning for closure
is not what I thought it would be.*

*Closure is not completion.
Nothing ends in my Afterloss.*

*Closure is being at peace with what
is left unsaid, undone, unfinished.*

I would go to those places where I could cry.
I would touch those tender places within me
and lean against the sharp edges surrounding me.
Where it hurt the most is where
I found the most healing.

Closure is not finality.
There is nothing final in loss.

Life does not begin with birth
and does not end with death.

Every season, everyone,
every moment,
closes into an opening.

*I am so grateful
for the ability to cry.*

*Every tear that has been
shaped by my heart,
by sorrow, finds its
way into my healing.*

*Each tear leads me
into the expanse.*

*Even though
my tears often hurt,
they always heal.*

Loss is not linear.

*The multi layers of my sorrow
take me deeper into places
that I never knew existed.*

*My steps go inward,
layer after layer,
not forward.*

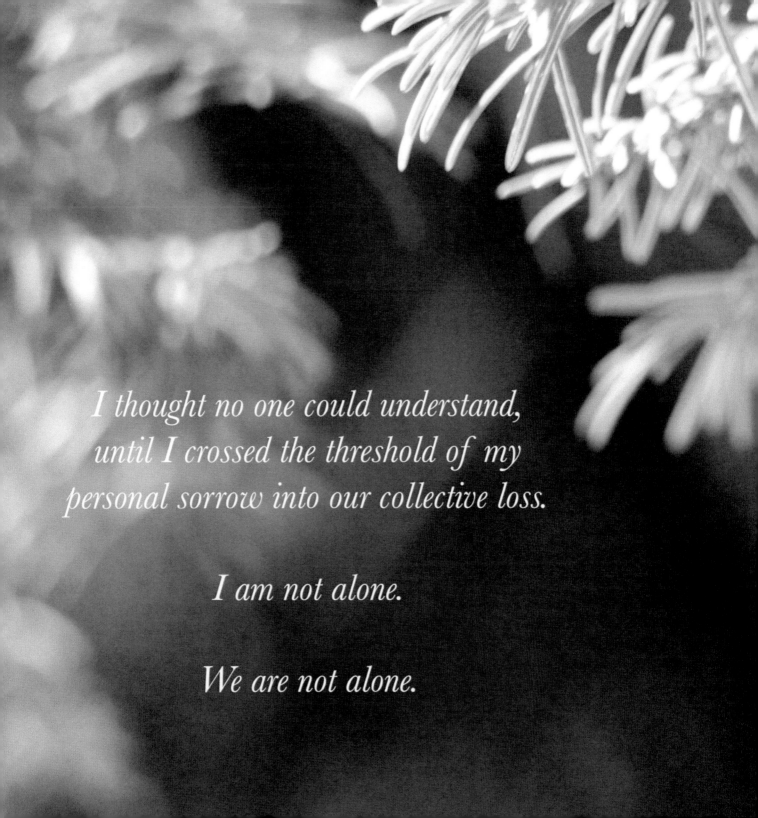

*I thought no one could understand,
until I crossed the threshold of my
personal sorrow into our collective loss.*

I am not alone.

We are not alone.

Summer

The slumbering days of Summer push Spring aside. My Autumn, Winter and Spring gather me under a sun that sits closer to my earth. The tides of my life are drawn closer to the lunar night, expanding and contracting far beyond the water beside me and the ocean within me.

Life has found a way to wed my moment into the "also" of my days. I embrace all of my life because I also embrace all of my loss. I will always love the ones I can no longer physically touch and I will also continue to experience the loss of that touch. They are still here and I am also gone. I am still here, yet I am also beyond here. I can go to places of memory and also be completely in the present. I am living in loss; I am also living in love; I am also living in life. I have gently settled into my "also" life in the Summer of my solace.

Living in loss has given me more, not less. Loss has brought me to the edge of the expanse. Every contraction into the greatest pain I've ever experienced has unfolded me into the expanse of the greatest love I could ever imagine. It has not been easy. It is not easy. Still, the season will move and I will move with it.

What ebbs will flow. What flows will ebb. Nothing in loss is linear. Loss, love and life come and go in the expanse. And there is no end point to my loss, just as there is no end point to my love. One moment I will be nestled in a harmonic peace. The next moment may shred me into the indescribable. Yet, as I lean into whatever arises, I am ready for whatever descends.

As I go deeper into my peace, I find the remnants of my sorrow. And as I go into the depths of my sorrow, I encounter the gentle resilience of my peace. What is there to give when so much has been taken? Nothing can replace what has been taken. I have no illusion that around some illusory corner I will be given back what is lost. Giving all I am to all that is, is not a replacement for all that was.

Giving is the very current of life itself. Just as Autumn, Winter, Spring and Summer give freely of themselves, I in turn, can give freely of myself to the world within me and the world around me. By giving all of me I find all of us.

The pain of separation in my loss has given way to the gratitude of an infinite embrace of connection in the midst of loss. The healing of my sorrow is not the eradication of my pain. My healing finds peace and purpose in the midst of loss. Loss has never stopped hurting, but that excruciating pain that paralyzed me has subsided into all of life, into all of death, into all that has no end – into love.

I did not go through all this to dissolve into nothing. I have traveled this path of loss, love and life to dissolve into everything. By letting go of everything, I am now able to let go into everything. Our life together taught me what love truly was. My life today is a testament of what love truly is. They did not die in vain. And I will not live in vain.

My here is no longer just here.

There is a part of me that no moment,
no Summer, no season can confine.

I feel the expanse of me reaching all
the way to you.

My heart into our heart.

I thought this pain would last forever.
Gratefully I was wrong.
It is the love that is lasting forever.

Healing is finding peace with the hurt.

*Healing is being able to hurt and finding
the expansion of my compassion and love
unfold through the tears.*

*Healing is touching those places that
touched me so deeply in tender gratitude.*

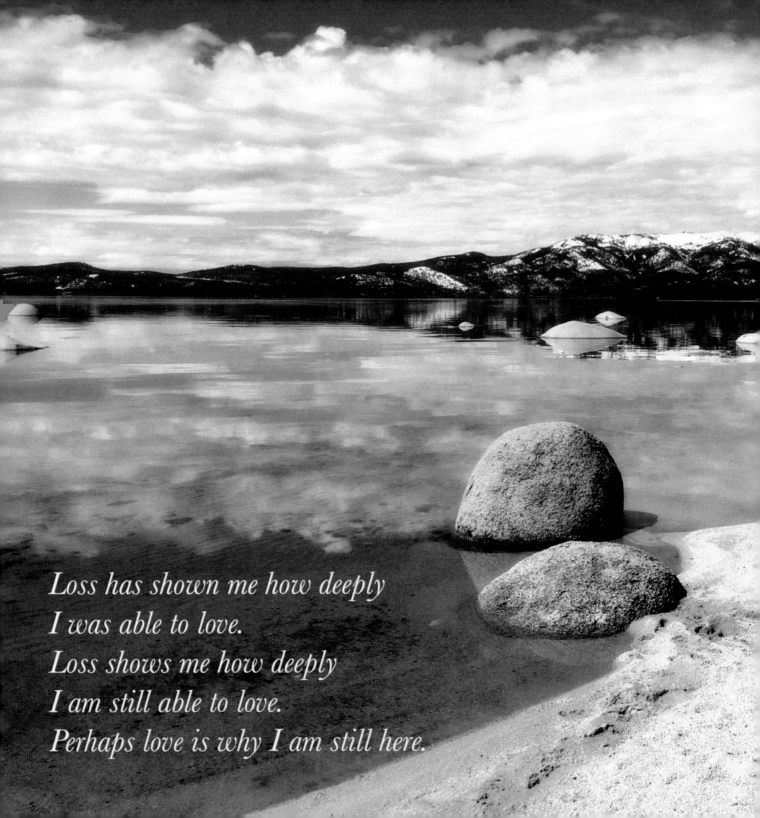

Loss has shown me how deeply
I was able to love.
Loss shows me how deeply
I am still able to love.
Perhaps love is why I am still here.

Everyone has a story to share.
And in the sharing, we heal.

I feel closer to me when
I am drawn closer to you.

What we have lost
can never be replaced,
but what we have left is our story,
and each other.

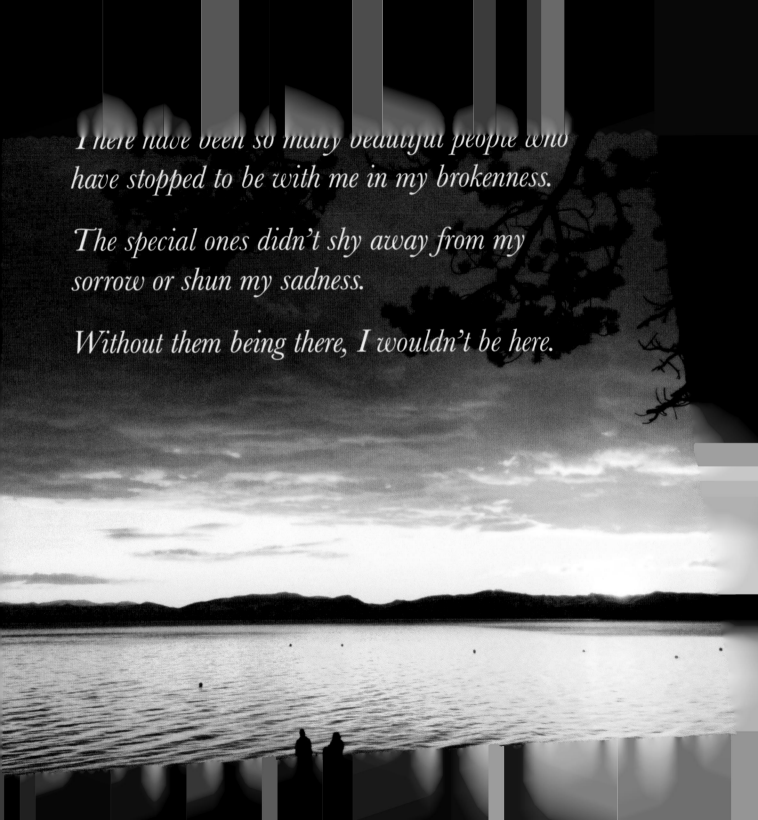

There have been so many beautiful people who have stopped to be with me in my brokenness.

The special ones didn't shy away from my sorrow or shun my sadness.

Without them being there, I wouldn't be here.

To miss the ones I love so deeply,
to feel the vacuum of my life
so powerfully,
yet to show up for my life,
says my love is a part of my loss
just as much as my loss
is a part of my love.

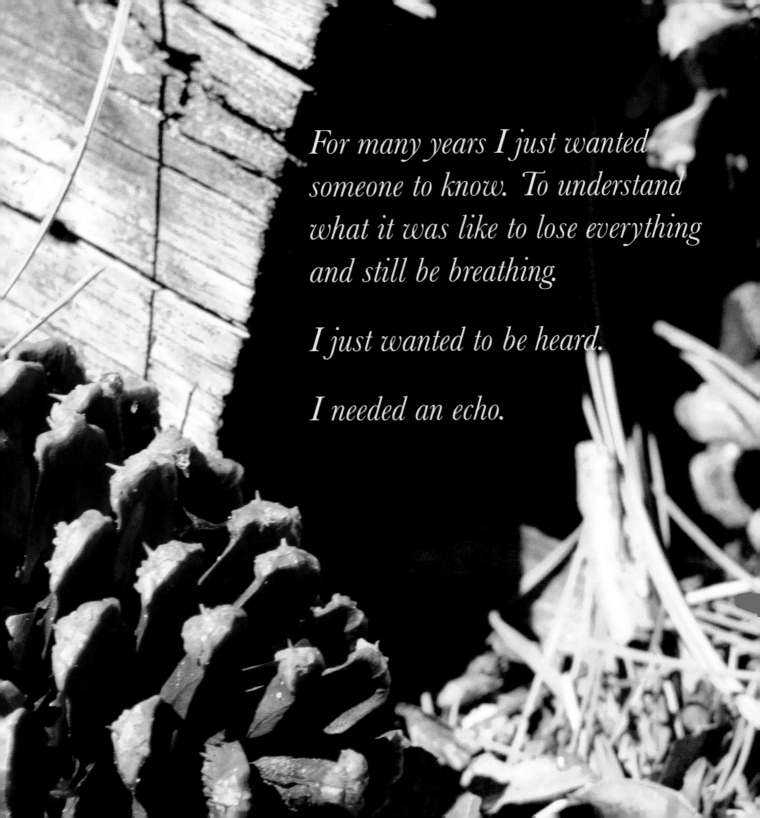

For many years I just wanted someone to know. To understand what it was like to lose everything and still be breathing.

I just wanted to be heard.

I needed an echo.

Sometimes I just wanted to stop,
but the world kept pulling me along.

I now know I needed that more
than I realized.

In my world of the Afterloss,
I've learned to accept that sometimes I
don't always know what I really need.

Nothing lives in isolation.

Not my loss, not my love.

Especially my love.

When I lose someone I love,
I need love more than ever.

The solitary nature of loss
cries out for another's presence.

In times of massive upheaval,
safe and supportive people harbor me,
hold me, heal me.

It was not love I needed to let go of.
It was love I needed to let go into.

Why would anybody say to another
not to cry?

Have you ever seen what happens to a
river that has no outlet?

The beautiful inner landscape of my life
has been carved by the tears that have
shaped my sorrow into solace,
my pain into presence,
my heart into our heart.

*One loss brings up all losses,
just as one love is a reflection of all love.*

Can I go through anything
and still love?

Can I keep my heart open
no matter how broken my heart is?

Can I wake up in the morning and ask,
"What can I give to life?"

They did not die in vain;
and I will not live in vain.

I feel their presence around me often.

But I feel their presence within me always.